Ireland

Peat, cut from the bogs that constitute over six percent of the country's surface, is the traditional Irish fuel; here, in southern Connemara, it is being laid out to dry.

Ireland

by DEREK A. C. DAVIES

Published by
KODANSHA INTERNATIONAL LTD.
Tokyo, Japan & Palo Alto, Calif., U.S.A.

Distributed in Continental Europe by Boxerbooks, Inc., Zurich; in Canada by Fitzhenry & Whiteside Limited, Ontario; and in the Far East by Japan Publications Trading Co., P.O. Box 5030 Tokyo International, Tokyo. Published by Kodansha International Ltd., 2-12-21 Otowa, Bunkyo-ku, Tokyo 112, Japan, and Kodansha International/U.S.A., Ltd., 599 College Avenue, Palo Alto, California 94306. Copyright © 1972, by Kodansha International Ltd. All rights reserved. Printed in Japan.

LCC 72-77797
ISBN 0-87011-180-9
JBC 0026-783569-2361

First edition, 1972

Contents

Dubliners and Saints

In Liverpool, this cloudy, blustery June morning, we fear a stormy passage as we board the car ferry, M.S. *Munster*, which has promised to deposit us in Dublin in some seven hours. The barman, who pours out the first Guinnesses of our Irish journey, confirms our fears, gloomily warning us that the Munster is long overdue for a bad crossing. But we consider ourselves fairly good sailors, so we are not particularly apprehensive as the ferry moves cautiously out to begin its crossing of the sometimes angry Irish Sea.

We have embarked, my wife and I, on a summer's motor trip through Ireland, our chief object being to photograph its ancient monuments, particularly those of the early Christian period, a time which, most people will allow, was Ireland's "Golden Age." We also plan to visit the bleak and beautiful west coast and some of the islands on the fringe of Europe, such as the Arans and the deserted Blaskets; nor will we consider our picture of Ireland complete if we omit the unhappy cities of the north, Londonderry and Belfast. The project appears, as we set out, a pleasant one for a summer's working holiday.

The ferry today seems packed to capacity: campers and caravan travelers with their assorted gear, fishermen toting rods and tackle,

IRELAND ♣

Irish laborers returning from English building sites and factories, a couple of priests (sitting, by God's grace, at the bar), a few specimens of that tweedy type of Anglo-Irish gentry that I thought had vanished from the earth long ago, and, from the look of them, those admirable people who go to Ireland just for the peace and quiet and who truly do not care if it rains all day every day of their stay, which it has been known to do.

The traveler is not allowed to forget that the tourist trade is one of Ireland's chief sources of income. On the paneled walls of the ship hang advertisements for hotels, for stately homes open to the visitor, for cars to rent, for shops of various sorts in Dublin. The ship's store displays Irish linen dish towels, leprechaun dolls, miniature gypsy caravans, blackthorn shillelaghs, and albums of Irish folk songs.

The signs on the toilet doors, I note, are lettered in Gaelic: *Fir* (for "Ladies") and *Mna* (for "Gentlemen"), a reminder of the pride the Irish take in their culture and language—and a reminder also that, strange as it seems, we are indeed going to a foreign country. We fall into conversation with a Dublin engineer, returning from a business trip to England, who explains that all children must learn Erse, or Irish Gaelic, in the national schools, although it is not used as the country's first language except in small areas on the west coast known as the Gaeltacht and within certain families who speak it as a matter of principle.

He himself, he tells us, has forgotten most of the Irish he once learned at school, nor does he need it in his job. The only time that he wished he remembered more of it was while he was on holiday on the west coast, where he found he was unable to speak to the locals at the pub. Even in the Dail (the Irish parliament), he points out, Irish is rarely spoken. He gives it as his opinion that the language is dying out and can never be reestablished as a living tongue. Then, unfortunately, our conversation shifts to politics and religion. I find that we are not in agreement, and that if one *must* discuss these subjects in Ireland, one should learn to tread as lightly as the leprechauns themselves.

Driving off the ferry onto Irish soil, we have no doubt that we are actually in a foreign country, and yet it is difficult to be sure why. The city, at first glance, resembles many English towns, except that the telephone booths, the post boxes, and the buses are cream and green rather than the brilliant red of England. And the police wear flat caps wholly unlike the imposing round helmets of the British bobby.

When we pull up and ask a passerby how to get to our hotel in Rathmines, we are answered with a question: "You're after coming from England?" Then the weather: "It's a grand day." "It is so." The Irish accent is soft and charming, and of course there can be no doubting the fact that the Irish talk a lot more than we do in England: they spend words like sailors on a spree while we English are said to hoard them like misers. By the time we have received minute instructions as to how to get from O'Connell Bridge to the Mount Herbert Hotel, we are wholly lost. Yet eventually we arrive.

Dublin is not a city that takes the breath away at first sight. There are few stately buildings, no wide tree-lined avenues, no great, spacious plazas. With a population of less than a million, it seems more like a large provincial town, the kind where a man can still drive out from the city center for lunch in the suburbs in twenty minutes or so. Less than ten years ago, we are told, there

9

were no speed limits in Dublin, and parking meters, which have been installed only recently, are blatantly ignored.

Cities, it seems to me, have characters, just as people have; Dublin I would describe as a favorite old aunt, a lady of great charm but of a certain mystery. Her clothes are faded and out of style and her views are definitely old-fashioned, yet she is as kind a soul as can be and has the knack of making any stranger feel at home—though she has been known to startle a new acquaintance by asking him point-blank whether he is a Protestant or a Catholic. She fascinates her visitor with stories of her youth in language as soft and rich as any he has ever heard; her tongue, however, when the need arises, can be as sharp as a broken bottle. And speaking of bottles, one must never forget there is nothing she likes better than her few pints of stout.

Of course, although our stay in the city is to be a short one, we visit a number of Dublin's pubs, starting off, logically enough, with Davy Bryne's Bar off Grafton Street. For those who recall *Ulysses*, it is the "Moral Pub," where James Joyce himself imbibed an occasional drink. Now it is all sleek furniture and dim lights, nothing like what it was when (in *Dubliners*) Farringdon found Nosey Flyn "sitting in his usual corner of Davy Bryne's."

At Jim Moran's, by the River Liffey, we encounter a white-haired old man wearing a black Homburg. The proprietor of a jewelry shop around the corner, he could be a character straight out of Joyce, sitting here at the bar telling jokes with all the style of a professional comedian in language that ought reasonably to have disappeared long ago. " 'Beghorra,' she screeched at himself, 'when you're dead I'll dance on your grave.' 'Sure, I don't mind at all,' replied himself—'I'll be having my funeral at sea!' "

Pausing briefly as the word "sea" gathers associations in his mind, the old man turns to me, the stranger: "You've heard of the Red Sea, have you?" I nod doubtfully, apprehensive about what might be coming next. "Well," he went on, "I painted it."

My mind makes its own associations. I think of the River Liffey outside, green and polluted, with its coating of black oil. Is it true, I ask, that Irish Guinness gets its fine taste, so much better than it is anywhere else in the world, from the Liffey water? "Sure, that's ridiculous," the old man replies indignantly. "The water comes through a pipe from a reservoir twenty-five miles away.

"There are," he continues reflectively, "seven million glasses of Guinness drunk each day in about twenty-five countries of the world. And I drink ten of them. I tell you, Ireland's the easiest country in the world. It's the only place I know of where you can go out to buy a box of matches and come home eight hours later—drunk." At that, he taps his glass on the long bar to attract the barman's attention and calls for another round. Then he continues, in a mellow, philosophical vein: "I don't have enough money to save or to spend on fine clothes and cars and houses, so that leaves me enough for the lady with the white top and the black skirt.... We're a Catholic country here, and a man's got to have an outlet. And that's why we drink more than most."

Another time, we make our way to Mulligan's in Poolbeg Street, another Joycean house which happily looks now much as it would have done to Farringdon when he ended his pub crawl here. It is snug and warm, with dark, paneled walls and white-aproned barmen, who pull the black porter lovingly from the taps. A pleasant hum of talk rises from a group of long-haired men, some of them, we are told, from the *Irish Press,* which is just around the corner.

IRELAND ♣

We get into conversation with a picture restorer named Paul Proud, who, giving substance to Ireland's proverbial hospitality, asks us to come and visit him in his flat in St. Stephen's Green, although he has only just met us. When the pub closes, sometime after eleven-thirty (by which time we are all a bit "mouldy," as they say in Dublin), we find his openhearted invitation very welcome. The next morning, a sober and suffering Paul, only half remembering who his guests are, tells us about St. Stephen's Green. It is one of the city's finest Georgian squares and many of her most famous sons were born here or lived nearby: Jonathan Swift, Thomas Moore, Oscar Wilde, Bernard Shaw, the Duke of Wellington, Daniel O'Connell, William Butler Yeats, to name but a few. Now, Paul says with a sigh, the square is mostly given over to doctors and dentists.

There can not be many old cities in the world whose three most important buildings of historic interest are a post office, a customs house, and a jail. In Dublin, all three were built around the turn of the nineteenth century, and all three have played their part in Ireland's long struggle for independence. Today they are recognized symbols of that struggle.

During the Easter Rising of 1916, Patrick Pearse and his small band of fighters made their headquarters in the General Post Office building and from it issued the manifesto proclaiming the Irish Free State, perhaps the most important single document in all of Irish history. Within the building stands a modern statue of Cú Chulainn, the Celtic hero who is another symbol of a free Ireland.

A statue of Daniel O'Connell, who fought for Catholic emancipation in the last century, stands not far away, in the same street. Around the plinth of the statue are angels in whose breasts may be seen bullet holes put there during the 1916 street fighting. It is suggestive to note that there are many statues of Irish revolutionaries to be found in Dublin but none of kings and queens, while the memorial to Lord Nelson, the English naval hero, was blasted by the Irish Republican Army (the I.R.A.) and has never been reerected. Blowing up statues does, in fact, seem to be a favorite political pastime here.

Five years after the Easter Rising, the I.R.A. captured the Customs House, burning much of it and thus destroying a number of important records. The act was a serious blow to the British administration. The stone has recently been restored, scrubbed as clean as bleached bone, and the building emerges as a splendid example of the Irish pseudo-classical style.

As for the jail, that is called Kilmainham and is now a museum of Ireland's struggle to achieve independence. As one goes through it, the guide explains that many of the country's revolutionary leaders were imprisoned and some were executed here: Emmet, Parnell, and Pearse, among others. Robert Emmet spent his last night at Kilmainham. It was he who, before his execution, wrote, "When my country takes her place among the nations of the earth, then, and not till then, let my epitaph be written." Charles Parnell, who died in 1891 and lies buried in Dublin, was imprisoned for seven months in Kilmainham. After the Easter Rising, the cells overflowed, and ninety-seven people were condemned to death. Of them, sixteen (including Pearse) were shot in the stone-breakers' yard before the sentences of the others were commuted to life imprisonment. In Yeats's words, the "terrible beauty" born out of this supreme sacrifice was destined to inspire and consolidate Ireland's determination to be free. It is a determination that still

grips the minds of Republicans on both sides of the border; and the dispassionate observer, I think, must inevitably reach the conclusion that Ireland can never be happy until she is a united and independent nation.

As we drive south from Dublin, we watch the dark clouds cast their shifting shadows over the Wicklow Mountains. The cutting of the turf has been finished only recently, and the oblong sods are stacked in glistening black "reeks," as they are called locally. By the time we reach Glendalough ("the Valley of the Two Lakes"), the site of an ancient monastery and the first stopping point on our journey into the past, the clouds have thickened; rain seems to hang motionless over the two lakes like a veil of lace. Perhaps this is how the ruins of the monastery, of any ancient monastery, should best be seen: the surrounding hills shrouded in mist, the old stones glistening, the pines dripping, with not another soul about to break the magic spell.

Several centuries before Europe's first universities were founded and long before Dublin, Cork, Galway, or any of the other big towns came into existence, large monastic communities like Glendalough flourished as centers of learning, literature, and the arts. This, between the sixth and the ninth centuries, was the Golden Age, when Ireland kept alive the flame of classical and Christian learning while much of the rest of Europe still floundered in the darkness that followed the fall of the Roman Empire of the West. Foreign scholars came to Ireland to study, and at the same time Irish monks ventured abroad, where they founded monasteries and schools to revive classical learning and to spread Christian doctrine, which had vanished with the barbarian invasions.

One of the colorful heroes of the age was St. Brendan, who

flourished during the sixth century. A monk who spent the last days of his life as abbot of a Benedictine monastery in eastern Galway, he is said to have undertaken a seven years' voyage in "a wicker boat with ox-skins covered o'er . . . in search of the land of promise of the saints." Among his many adventures (which included a meeting with Judas Iscariot, who happened to be sitting atop an iceberg in a storm-tossed sea, and making a landing on a whale which the good saint mistook for an island), there is the remarkable claim that he actually got as far as the American mainland. In support of this allegation, investigators adduce the fact that crosses and beehive huts of similar type and age are to be found on both sides of the Atlantic. If there is any truth to the legend and the theory, then America was discovered by an Irish monk nearly a thousand years before Columbus reached it.

A contemporary of St. Brendan, St. Kevin was the founder of Glendalough, which, like so many monasteries of the time, began its existence as the refuge of a single hermit monk. St. Kevin, so the story goes, lived in a small cave on the cliff face high above the upper lake. After a time, he gained fame as a man of great saintliness and was joined by a community of monks. Upon Kevin's death, Glendalough became a center of pilgrimage until, by the twelfth century, it had become what the historian Liam de Paor calls a monastic "pseudo-city."

In their day, the monks of Glendalough built small stone churches, high stone crosses, a round stone tower, and wooden huts. The huts have of course, long since disappeared, and the churches (with the single exception of the tiny, beautiful structure known as St. Kevin's Kitchen) are now in ruins, destroyed and plundered during the Viking invasions of the eighth and ninth centuries; but the round tower has survived and is not only the best preserved but also probably the most harmoniously proportioned in all of Ireland. These towers, strange pencil-shaped structures that are such a common feature of the Irish landscape, are thought to have been built both as bell towers to call the faithful to prayer and also for defensive purposes. The doors of the towers are usually placed about ten feet above ground, which would enable the monks to take refuge inside during an invasion, afterward pulling up the ladder by which they had entered.

In addition to the hours devoted to prayer, most of the monks would have worked, some in the fields, others as craftsmen of various kinds. The filigree work and book illumination of the Irish monks were of unsurpassed excellence. Two fine examples of the latter are the Book of Kells and the Book of Durrow, treasures which have survived the centuries and may now be seen at the library of Trinity College, Dublin.

Before the momentous arrival of Ireland's patron saint in the fifth century, her people, like most people in the world at the time, were unlettered: unable either to read or to write, they depended for the perpetuation of their rich store of myth and saga on the court bards (called *filli*), who often required as much as twenty years of training in order to commit all the various legends to memory. There was, to be sure, a simple form of writing known as *Ogham,* which was used to carve inscriptions on stone, but it was impractical for anything longer than a few words. To incise the average modern novel in Ogham would require a stone about a mile high.

With St. Patrick came Christianity, and with Christianity came the Roman script. It was only then that the ancient Celtic literature

1-2. *Dublin*, the capital, has many fine ▶
Georgian houses: *opposite*, Merion
Square; *: overleaf*, the city's heart—the
River Liffey,   and the bridge, monu-
ment, and street   named   for   Daniel
O'Connell.

IRELAND ☘

was written down for the first time, either by the monks themselves
(who were apt to make alterations to conform to the new faith)
or by lay scholars who had learned their writing from the monks.
Despite the inevitable corruptions, these early written works,
repeated through the centuries, have provided today's scholars who
are investigating Ireland's ancient history with invaluable material.

As the Vikings increased their incursions into Ireland, some
centuries later, the writing and illumination of manuscripts as well
as metalwork fell into decline probably because the artists and
craftsmen had no strong desire to create things that could be carried
away as plunder. Along with the decline came the increased pro-
duction of high crosses, whose size and weight made them impossible to take away. Interestingly, many of the designs and motifs
of the metalworkers were carved into the sandstone or granite of
the earlier crosses; later ones were decorated mostly with biblical
scenes.

As we wander about the empty ruins, examining the crumbling
churches, the old crosses, and the inscriptions on the gravestones,
we think back to the days when Glendalough was a kind of Irish
Rome, when the now deserted valley hummed with the energies of
hundreds of men, praying, studying, and working. Now the focus of
time has shifted; today's equivalent of the men of Glendalough are
university professors and doctors of medicine and industrial
scientists; but the worn old stones still stand, and a spirit of holiness
permeates still the soft misty air.

3. *Grafton Street*, which is an important shopping center, is reflected in a store window displaying Ireland's well-known Waterford crystal and showing a mock-Georgian façade.

4. *Madigan's* in Earl Street: "Tempus Fugit" reads the notice below the clock, to which the Irish reply, "He who made time made plenty of it."

6. *Jerpoint Abbey*, one of the country's finest monastic ruins, dates from the Middle Ages, when a new spirit of Christianity was sweeping across Ireland.

5. *Glendalough Monastery*, mostly in ruins, was founded in the sixth century and until the twelfth century flourished as a center of arts and learning.

25

7. *Round towers*, built between the tenth and twelfth centuries, are common features of the Irish countryside; they served both as bell towers and as defenses against the invading Vikings. This tower is at Clonmacnois.

8-9. *High Cross (left)* and Cross of the Scriptures *(above)*, both at Clonmacnois: the latter is generally considered to be the finest of the country's many high crosses; thirteen feet tall, it depicts a number of Biblical scenes.

27

10. *Rock of Cashel* overlooks Tipperary's rich and
fertile Golden Vale. It was here that St. Patrick
preached the doctrine of the Trinity, using the

shamrock as an illustration and giving Ireland
her national emblem. The round tower dates from
around the tenth century.

11. *Red hair* is commonest among tinkers, although, contrary to popular opinion, only about four percent of the entire population of Ireland is carrot-topped.

12-13. *Itinerant tinkers*, the Irish version of gypsies, are a familiar sight. Not of Romany blood, some are descended from the wandering craftsmen of ancient Ireland, others from families dispossessed of their land. Formerly tinsmiths, they now eke out their living trading in scrap and the like.

14. *A cooperative* at Kilcrohane in County Cork, where in the early morning farmers bring milk to be converted into butter, cheese, and other dairy products.

15-16. *Cork*, most Irish of cities, is the second largest in the republic, a major seaport and industrial center. *Opposite*, the view from the belfry of St. Ann's Church, famous for its old bells. *Below*, St. Patrick's Street crosses the River Lee at St. Patrick's Bridge and goes up St. Patrick's Hill.

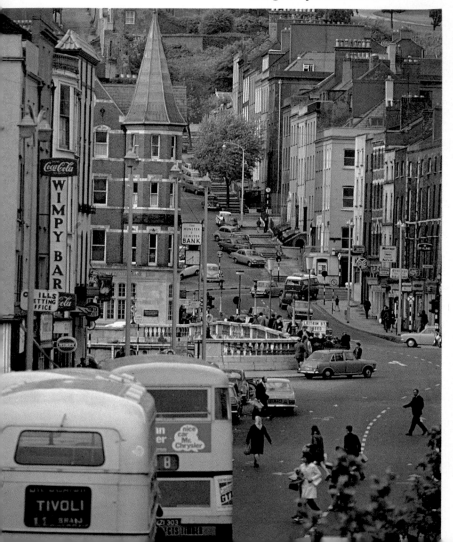

17-21. *Puck Fair*, at Kilorglin in County Kerry, is one of the country's oldest, dating back to pagan times. A goat (*right*) is crowned king and hoisted atop a scaffold in the main square (*left*) to survey three days of festivities. Card games (*lower right*), though illegal, are popular at races and fairs. An onlooker (*lower left*), separates two farmers about to come to blows over the price of a horse. Country horse fairs (*below*), such as this one at Kenmare in County Kerry, are still important social occasions for farmers but are largely being replaced by modern cattle markets.

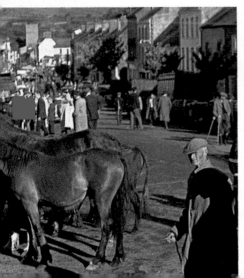

22. *Long sandy beaches* skirting Ireland's lovely coastline
offer superb terrain for horseback riding.

23. *Stone circles*, of pagan origin, were used by the druids for religious ceremonies; this one is at Drombeg, County Cork.
24. *The twin-faced statue* (*above*), on Boa Island, County Fermanagh, is another reminder of Ireland's pagan past.

25. *Cursing stones*, like the one near Kenmare (*above right*), were first used as grinding stones and only later became associated with black magic.

26. *Holy wells* (*right*), also pre-Christian, are now named after Christian saints—this one, in Armagh, for St. Patrick.

27. *Lakes of Kilarney*, Ireland's most famous scenic wonder, inspired Brendan Behan to remark that it would be impertinent to attempt to extol them.

The Celtic Isles

From Glendalough we drive southwest, following an itinerary worked out on the basis of Peter Harbison's *Guide to the National Monuments of Ireland* (Gilly Macmillan, 1970). In addition to the early Christian period, I am also particularly interested in the prehistory of the country. The bridge between that past and the present is broken forever, though as we travel through the countryside we see considerable evidence of those lost years: standing stones, dolmens, stone circles, megalithic tombs, stone forts. Nobody knows exactly why some of them were built, or what ceremonies were performed about them, and nobody can ever be sure. The mystery must always remain, and with it the fascination.

Scholars do, of course, have some knowledge of this early period. They think that probably the first human beings crossed to the island around the beginning of the sixth millennium B.C. The land was richly forested, and the firstcomers were hunters, who have left behind few tokens of their existence except rubbish heaps, hearths, and some very primitive tools. Then, around 3000 B.C., during the Late Stone Age, farming was introduced. Sedentary now, people began the construction of more enduring monuments. Huge megalithic tombs, such as those at Newgrange and Knowth, built around this time, are among the finest in Europe. Of varying types, some are located within large round mounds, others under massive stone dolmens. The tombs of the Boyne Valley area include stones that are decorated in strange and beautiful designs, the symbolic meaning of which may now only be imagined.

The ancient Irish seem to have had a stong feeling for stones, particularly those of phallic shape, which the people would stand upright as a primitive form of sculpture. These may have been used to mark boundaries or battlegrounds or burial sites. Those which were inscribed in Ogham must have been gravestones. Some that have been found are splendidly decorated, notably the Turoe stone near Galway, which is ornamented with the Celtic La Tene design.

As the Stone Age became Bronze, some time after 2000 B.C., native Irish artists quickly developed a remarkable taste and skill, evidence of which may now be seen in the beautiful gold ornaments displayed in the National Museum in Dublin. Perhaps the most noteworthy piece is a gold *lunula,* a form of necklace made in the shape of a crescent moon. During the period between 1700 and 600 B.C. Ireland was something of a European El Dorado, and there is evidence that Irish gold was traded as far away as Egypt and the Near East.

After bronze and gold came iron, which was brought to the country by the Celts. These powerful and aggressive warriors, with their superior iron weapons, originated in Central Europe but soon spread as far west as Spain, as far east as Asia Minor, where they established the colony of Galatia. The various Celtic tribes, whom the Greeks called *keltoi,* seem to have spoken a common language, but they never established a unified empire like that of the Romans, nor did they possess any sort of central organization. They

44

did not even build cities; they were an illiterate and nomadic people, but they were renowned for their eloquence and bravery.

Around 400 B.C. they plundered Rome and Sicily, and in the third century they invaded Greece. Around the same time, they crossed to Ireland, bringing with them social institutions, a language, and a character type that the country has retained, to a certain extent, to this very day. It was primarily people of Celtic stock who were converted to Christianity by St. Patrick in the fifth century: present-day Ireland's deepest roots, then, are to be found in the ancient Celts and in early Christianity.

IRELAND ♣

At Castledermot, we stop to photograph a ruined Franciscan friary and several of the high crosses. The Franciscans as well as other monastic orders from the continent (the Augustinians, the Dominicans, and the Cistercians) established themselves in Ireland in the twelfth and thirteenth centuries, at a time when the older Irish monasteries had lost much of their original purpose and a new spirit of Christianity was sweeping across Europe. The round tower of Castledermot is a fine one, but the friary, like so much else in Ireland, was almost totally destroyed by Cromwell. Where once monks intoned their prayers screeching black crows now build their nests.

In a field near Browneshill we come upon a massive stone dolmen around which peacefully grazes a large herd of cows. Consisting of several standing stones roofed over with a huge capstone, this and other dolmens of the same type are in fact tombs dating from the Bronze Age, although Irish legend insists that they were beds used by two young lovers, Diarmaid and Gráinne, fleeing the wrath of a jealous king.

Making our way through a muddy farmyard at Moone, we come upon an exquisite high cross from whose carvings the faces of twelve dwarflike apostles stare wistfully out. Then, further south, near Carrick-on-Suir, after a tortuous drive through a jungle of country lanes, we encounter the high crosses of Ahenny. Elaborately decorated with Celtic motifs, these crosses, which have weathered a thousand years of wind and rain in this quiet corner of rural Ireland, are among the oldest and finest in the country. We are assured by an elderly man tending the graves that the crosses have stood there "since the first people woke up in the morning."

The approach to the Rock of Cashel on the wide, lush plain of the Golden Vale of Tipperary is among the most dramatic and moving sights in all of Ireland. The great stone fortress stands haughtily on a limestone outcrop that commands the country for miles around. Although its name sounds strangely like that of some middle-eastern sheikdom, the Rock of Cashel was the center of power in southern Ireland as early as the fourth century, when it was used as a fortress by the kings of Munster. When St. Patrick visited Cashel, he expounded the doctrine of the Trinity by making use of a three-leaf clover; this is the source, according to legend, of Ireland's national emblem, the shamrock. Other powerful and royal names are associated with Cashel: in 977 Brian Boru, the first king of all Ireland was crowned here, after which he made it his capital; in the twelfth century, King Henry II of England visited Cashel; and a century later, King Robert I of Scotland, "the Bruce," convened a parliament on the rock.

The guide who shows us around the historic buildings has a more than adequate explanation as to why such an odd chunk of rock should find itself in the midst of a wide and fertile plain. "See that range of mountains over there," he says, pointing into the hazy distance. "You'll notice there seems to be a piece missing from the ridge. Well, the devil flew over and took a bite but didn't like the taste, so he dropped it on the plain here—and then flew back to his home in England."

They say there is a story behind every stone in Ireland, of which probably the best known is that which concerns the stone at Blarney Castle, near Cork. Many years ago, according to the story, a man was cursed with a stutter that no one could cure until a witch hung him by his legs outside the battlements of the castle, telling him to kiss a stone on the outer wall; he did, and he was cured, perhaps as a result of the shock. For a long time thereafter those who sought the gift of eloquence underwent the same perilous ordeal, but now it is possible to kiss the stone through a hole in the floor of the tower—there are stout steel bars as well as a guard to catch you should you slip. Although it is rather an unpleasant experience, the castle is visited every year by thousands of people who hope to receive the gift of gab in return for a kiss. As we leave Cashel, we wonder whether its guide was one of those who made the pilgrimage to Blarney.

Ireland, we decide, would be a paradise for motorists were it not for the occasional driver who gives one the impression he has never driven before, and were it not also for the herds of cows that drift casually down the middle of the road. Though sometimes rather narrow and not always well surfaced, roads lead almost everywhere, even to very remote corners of the country, and are often quite deserted, even at the height of the tourist season.

Irish mechanics, we find, are excellent. We are driving an old Ford Consul convertible, the like of which I am never to encounter in Ireland, although saloon Consuls (as well as other vehicles which would be obsolete elsewhere) are common enough here. In Ireland old cars never die, even if they have to be tied together now and then with bits of string. On one occasion a mechanic carrying out a minor repair for us refuses to take any money: "Not at all, 'tis not'ing," he says. "I'm glad to be helping a fine old car like her back on the road."

We stop at sleepy country villages with names like Ballyhooly and Belgooly, where almost every other house is a combined pub and general store and where, at all hours of the day, the tempo is that which one associates with the lazy part of an afternoon. Down the gray main street ambles a donkey drawing a cart filled with milk cans, and with it drifts a mixed aroma of stale beer and soda bread, of cattle and turf.

As for the village pubs, whatever failings they may have in food and décor they make up for with blarney. Indeed, the visitor may decide with a certain amount of justification, that the Irish do very little but talk, and talk about any subject under the sun—as well as some beyond the stars. At one small village pub, forgetting my firm resolution to avoid religion, I suddenly find myself in danger of being hit over the head with a bottle of beer in an attempt to change my mind about the nature of the supreme deity. I save myself from this form of persuasion by recalling Spinoza's definition of God as nature. I reaffirm my resolution never to forget that Ireland is indeed a Catholic country.

On the walls of the pubs hang pictures of local Gaelic football and hurling teams as well as prints of revolutionary heroes like Tone and Emmet and Pearse. Photographs of the American Kennedys also frequently adorn Irish walls, for the Irish like to boast of their American cousins. In a pub near Listowel we see a "WANTED

IRELAND ♣

DEAD OR ALIVE" notice for Jessie James, who is something of a hero with the local people, for his parents were born there. At Mountshannon we are informed that the actor George Brent and the gambler "Legs" Diamond were both born in the village (that, in fact, they were half-brothers, the latter being the illegitimate son of the local swell). But the Irish, we have learned, are great leg-pullers, so we have no idea whether to believe this one or not.

We find, as we travel, that we most enjoy putting up at farm-houses for the night. It is not that there is any shortage of good accommodation; recent emphasis on tourism has inaugurated a minor boom in hotel building, so that even during the season the traveler can usually get a room without prior booking; and bed-and-breakfast houses are numerous and clean as well as being reasonably priced at less than three dollars a night. But we find the best value to be the farmhouses, and we also find them the most enjoyable.

They are easy to locate, for the Irish Tourist Board and the Farmhouse Association publish a list of the many families who put up visitors during the season. A night's lodging costs about the same as at a city house, but the breakfast is a stupendous one of "rashers and eggs." Twenty-five dollars or so will cover a week's bed-and-breakfast plus the evening meal—as well as the opportunity to lend a hand with the milking or the hay-making if a man feels inclined that way. The evening meal frequently features salmon or sea trout, for good fishing is available almost everywhere in Ireland. It is, in fact, one of the country's chief tourist attractions, and the Tourist Board has estimated that a salmon caught by a visitor brings into the country about thirty times more money than one caught commercially and sold for export.

The evenings we spend at farmhouses are many and pleasant. At

50

Mrs. Ryan's, near Kilkenny, we happily sing songs with the other guests late into the night. Mrs. Malone, formerly a professional singer in Dublin, does some old Gaelic songs for us, so poignant and sad we are near to tears; then, the moment she is finished singing, she is all smiles and laughter, cracking jokes and telling stories. I feel that there is something peculiarly Irish in this volatile mixture of intense joy and sorrow.

A memorable feature of travel in Ireland is its gypsies—or tinkers, as they are called—whose roadside camps we pass frequently as we move along. Their transport will consist of a couple of brightly painted horse-drawn caravans, perhaps a trailer pulled by an old car, and a few carts and horses. Around a campfire, washing is spread out to dry on the hedgerows; hungry-looking mongrel dogs wander about. If we stop for a moment, a swarm of grubby-faced children will descend on us, whining "A few coppers, spare a few coppers."

Tinkers used to earn their meager livings as tinsmiths, but widespread use of plastic buckets and mass-produced kitchenware has pretty much put an end to even this modest source of income. So now Ireland's tinkers deal in scrap and do casual farm work, supplementing their income with beggary and (according to reputation) petty thievery. Some have preferred to emigrate.

Although the fact has been established that few (if any) of them are actually of Romany blood, their origin remains uncertain. Many, it is thought, are descended from families evicted from their land by hardhearted landlords, others from ancient Ireland's wandering Celtic craftsmen. They speak, people say, a secret language of their own derived from that of the druids; at the same time, according to a government study of itinerants, they are almost wholly illiterate.

IRELAND ♣

They tend to marry young: about forty percent of female itinerants marry under the age of eighteen while the figure for the rest of Irish women is less than two percent. Their marriages are also more stable and are likely to result in more children than the Irish average. Sometimes the newspapers speak of a tinker "king," which would suggest that the tinkers still adhere to a form of chiefdom like that of the old Scots and Irish clans, but in fact tinker "kings" turn out to be no more than respected heads of large families—kings whose royalty exists only on newsprint.

At Cork, the republic's second largest city, we decide to make our stay as short as possible: it is industrialized and crowded, and the weather is disheartening. Besides, we are eager to get on to the west coast. We do take time, however, to climb the belfry of St. Anne's Church, Shandon, and look out over the gray mosaic of the city's slate roofs. As the famous old bells peal out, it is not difficult to recall that Cork in the eighteenth century was a major trading port, where sailors came in from the sea with strange tales of unexplored lands and unknown peoples, where frigates and cutters berthed along what is now the city's main street. I recall also that during the War of Independence of 1919–21 two lord mayors of Cork gave their lives for their country.

Still within County Cork, we continue on down the coast to Kinsale, another seaport of considerable historic interest. In 1601 a Spanish fleet sailed into the harbor, occupied the city, and tried to hold it against the English forces but failed despite Irish help. Under the English, the city became an important naval base and still today possesses an English flavor, partly because of some fine old Georgian houses, partly because it is much favored by English tourists, paticularly those who are interested in shark fishing and can afford the hire of boats, which are more expensive in Kinsale than elsewhere along the coast.

From the photographer's point of view Kinsale has the added attraction of being one of the very few places in Ireland where the long black cape is still worn. Presumably, however, the old women who wear the capes resent begin treated as objects of curiosity, for the minute they spot a camera they scurry away. Another interesting, if not world-shaking, piece of information in connection with the town is the fact that the present baron of

IRELAND ♣

Kinsale, the thirty-third in succession and Ireland's most senior baron, holds the unique privilege of keeping his hat on his head in the presence of royalty.

Driving westward from Kinsale, we follow the rugged and beautiful coastline of West Cork and Kerry, spending the nights when we can on the lovely beaches—wide, clean, and empty. Our only complaint is the coldness of the water. One morning, on a rocky beach at Akahista, on the Beara peninsula, I am awakened around five by a brilliant sun rising over the distant hills and bounding across Dunmanus Bay like a gunshot. Cries of sea birds furnish the sound track for this dramatic sunrise, which, however commonplace it may be in this part of the world, is a magical event for a city dweller like me. On a beach at Glenbeigh we watch horses galloping as if across a desert. Near Tralee, on a night when there are as many stars as the souls of the dead, we draw giant pictures in the sand and with the dawn watch the tide wash them away.

Another night, on a beach near Balinskelligs, we have a somewhat more exciting experience—one that could happen nowhere else in the world, I suppose, but Ireland. Our intention is to camp on the beach, but we stop first at the local pub. There we encounter a very drunk and very persistent character named Mike Murphy who, after telling us a long string of extremely dirty and not very funny jokes, insists that we accompany him to his house for "a drop more of the hard stuff" and a bed for the night. With great difficulty we refuse—and soon wish we had not, for the moment we approach the beach we find that our car has got firmly stuck in the sand.

With a rising tide, I estimate that we have about three hours to get the vehicle clear. Should we try to borrow a tractor from a local farmer? We have serious doubts, however, about the willingness of local farmers to lend out their tractors at midnight, so we decide to try to dig the car out ourselves. For two hours we work like slaves, using our cooking pots to shovel sand out from under the chassis. When at last it is clear, we put the tent under the back wheels and spare clothes under the front. I start the engine and let in the clutch. The wheels spin, and spin, and spin—and the car sinks ever deeper into the sand.

At this nightmarish moment, we suddenly hear another car approaching. It stops at the edge of the beach, its headlights catch us in the glare like dazzled rabbits, and out of the car roll Mike Murphy and a burly companion, both of them howling with laughter. They are carrying long gravediggers' spades, and Mike waves a shotgun in the air.

"It's to shoot the local constable, poor fellow," says Mike. "We wouldn't want him to disturb us now, would we?"

Before I have time to decipher this rather ambiguous question, the two men are working under my car, digging furiously. When the sand is cleared away, we attach a rope to Mike's car; I breathe a prayer to the Celtic gods—and we are free.

But the night, we find, is not yet over. It seems that ever since the pub closed, Mike and his friend Tim have been at Mike's house, having a nip, and after a time it seemed to them only reasonable that they should go out into the night to bury a dead beast that Mike calls a sea serpent. It is lying on the beach, he says, stinking to high heaven and creating a nuisance for everyone in the neighborhood, including a group of nuns who are on holiday in a nearby beach house. It occurs to me that Mike may have anticipated our disaster and out of the kindness of his heart come to help us, but of course I do not give voice to this supposition.

IRELAND ♣

Having had our car preserved from the incoming tide, we can do no more in return than attend the burial of the sea serpent. We drive some two hundred yards along the hard strand to a spot where there does indeed fester the putrid carcass of an animal of some sort. It is about twelve feet long, with a narrow skull, a vertebral column, and no limbs. Its entrails are spilled out onto the sand, and it is thick with flies. Is it a shark? A small whale? A porpoise? It looks like none of these. We decide that we agree with Mike and Tim: it can only be a sea serpent.

For the second time in the small hours of the morning, the two men are hard at work with their long spades. I marvel at their energy, which I suspect comes straight out of the bottle. Suddenly Mike thrusts the shotgun at me. "Fire both barrels," he says, "as we roll her in. 'Tis the last salute." With a double crash, certainly loud enough to wake the poor local constable, the sea serpent tumbles into its grave.

Back at Mike's house, an obvious bachelor's mess that he shares with a couple of dozen animals of various sorts, we celebrate the night's activities with a drink made of sugar, sherry, hot water, and poteen, that famous but illicit home-brewed whiskey of the west of Ireland that warms a man down to the tips of his toenails.

If the breathtakingly beautiful countryside is reason enough for coming to Ireland, the weather offers equally good cause for staying away. When it is good, it is very, very good; but when it is bad (which is all too often), it is indeed horrid. A bright smiling morning sun tricks the visitor into thinking the day will be a fine one; he goes off for a walk and in half an hour finds himself in the midst of a downpour. It is this unpredictability that makes Ireland's charm so fleeting and unsubstantial. Painters, for instance, find the landscape almost impossible to capture because the colors vary from minute to minute, and one photographer who came to take pictures of the beauties of Killarney stayed for a fortnight but because of the constant rain was unable to take one decent photograph.

Writers too are affected by the conditions under which they view a place—and not only meteorological conditions either. Beauty, we are assured, is in the eye of the beholder, and if the beholder happens to find himself standing ankle-deep in orange peel and surrounded by a hundred other people snapping away with their cameras, then he will probably decide to look for his beauty elsewhere. This, more or less, is our first impression of the Lakes of Killarney as seen from Ladies View, those lakes which Brendan Behan says it would be impertinent to praise and which leave even copywriters wordless. After camping overnight at Ladies View, however, we see the lakes at dawn and conclude that they well deserve their reputation.

Later, we take a side road into Black Valley, where the Mully-cuddy Reeks sweep down into the glen in majestic curves and where waterfalls etch the bare rock. Green fields seem to have been thrown across the coarse bog grass like rugs, here and there stands a white farmhouse, and sheep wander over the hills and valleys in shifting patterns of white dots. In places, rough gray rocks thrust upward through the earth like the fists of giants or the fins of buried dinosaurs: I no longer wonder at the host of strange legends Ireland has nurtured.

We decide to try to climb to the top of Carrantouhill, which, at 3,414 feet, is the country's highest mountain. The day began clear, but by the time we near the foot of the mountain, we find its peak closely wrapped in clouds. An old lady at a nearby farm tells us that some tourists perished recently after getting lost in the mist. So we content ourselves with stopping by the shore of Lake Curraghmore, where we listen to the water lapping at the stones, to the distant bleeting of the sheep, and to the silence. That silence is one of the reasons people come to Ireland.

In a remote valley beneath Mangatron Mountain, near Kilgarvan, we encounter a number of young Londoners who are living in an abandoned farmhouse. They exist almost entirely on their own efforts: they grow vegetables, cut turf, keep livestock, churn butter, bake bread. The nearest village is a five-hours' walk away. Living on the land is a challenge to them, justifying a way of life uncontaminated by industrialized urban society. But I wonder how well they will survive the long hard winters. Will they stay on here at the head of a glen so remote that even the local farmers have fled it? Or will they soon drift back to the city to earn their bread less arduously?

Near Kilgarvan we stay at Mrs. Traynor's farm, advertised in the Farm Holidays Association booklet as "a pleasant old-style farm house in attractive sylvan setting with mountains in background. Wide scope for the artist amongst these scenic surroundings." The problem is that there is not much scope for my wife to do her illustrations, because the rooms are too small to work comfortably in and there is no suitable table available. But the salmon that Mrs. Traynor serves us for dinner, fresh from the Roughty River behind the farmhouse, is superb. One evening I sit beside the bank, hoping to spot some otters and watching the surrounding mountains turn from dark green to black. The sound of the water breaking over the shallows is like the murmur of a thousand whispers.

Down the road toward Kenmare we stay with the O'Sullivans in a huge, rambling, salmon pink mansion which has obviously come down in the world. It is the sort of place that once boasted fine horses and that now survives only by taking in paying guests. The old mistress of the house creeps about trying to avoid us, and when that fails she pretends not to see us. John O'Sullivan works in the local library during the day and looks after his cows in the evening. His wife, Pat, who says "he who made time made plenty of it," is a fay Irish soul with a wicked sense of humor. Admiring a huge caldron outside her kitchen, I remark that it once must have been used for boiling missionaries. "You mean for boiling Englishmen," she replies.

Exploring the surroundings of Kenmare, we come upon a cursing stone that overlooks a beautiful valley far from the main road and the tourist routes. Such stones were apparently used originally for communal grinding; their cursing function seems to have come later. Several hollows were carved into a flat stone, and in each of the hollows was a smaller stone, of a size easily held in the hand. This was used to crush and grind the grain, or, turned three times against the direction of the sun while the turner repeated the name of an enemy, to transmit a curse.

This particular stone, obviously, has not often been visited by tourists, for the little round stones are still in their hollows. Although, so far as I know, cursing stones are no longer used, this one, I learn at a nearby farm, possesses an unsavory reputation. It seems that there was a local witch who was caught stealing milk and butter, so the neighboring farmers put a curse on her and turned both her and the butter she was carrying into stone. Once a man tried to carry the stone away, but the bridge over the river could not bear the weight of his cart with the stone in it. The bridge collapsed, and the man was drowned. We refrain from testing the stone's power, for we have been told that if a man curses someone without justification the curse recoils on the curser. And we can think of no one whom we may justifiably curse.

The stone circles we are looking for are tucked away in the most hard-to-find places, so we spend a lot of time asking directions. "And be sure not to sit on the stones," says one man to us, "for you'll be turned into leprechauns if you do." Another tells us: "The artiologists [sic] dug up the body of a small child from the middle of the circle, so they did, and they had a party there in the deep of the night with drinking and singing." He imparts this information with a sinister gleam in his eye, as though those "artiologists" had been engaging in some evil and heathenish rite. As a matter of fact, the circles were used by the druids, the aristocratic Celtic priestly caste, for ritualistic purposes.

Another reminder of pre-Christian Ireland are the holy wells, of which there are said to be several hundred scattered over the country. Many now are named after members of the vast communion of Irish saints, and people still come to the wells seeking cures for various ailments, just as they did in ancient Ireland, tying rags and pieces of string to nearby thorn trees as tokens.

Even the Irish passion for pilgrimages is not entirely of Christian origin. The pagan Irish, considering certain mountains to be sacred, held ceremonies on their summits, while today the best-known Irish pilgrimage is the annual ascent of Croak Patrick, St. Patrick's mountain. Thousands of pilgrims, some of them barefoot, climb it on one night each year and in the morning hear mass said on the peak. Another important place of pilgrimage is the island monastery in Loch Derr, in Donegal, to which visitors must come with a repentant spirit. While there, they walk barefoot, live on bread and

water, and pray through the night. Journalists and photographers are strenuously discouraged.

Lourdes is also much venerated in Ireland, and newspapers seem to be constantly carrying advertisements for package-tour pilgrimages to the French town. The English magazine *Punch* claims there are always vacant beds to be had in Irish hospitals, because belief in faith healing is so strong an Irishman will hop over to Lourdes if he so much as catches a bad cold.

Christianity, in any case, has never altogether displaced the culture and religion of the pagan Celts. "Christ is my druid," said St. Columba, suggesting the manner in which Christian ideas were joined to earlier traditions. Today Ireland is for the most part a devoutly Catholic country, although at the same time pre-Christian traditions survive, rather as in Japan ancient native Shintoism exists alongside later imported Buddhism, and people pay their respects to both.

28. *The Skelligs* lie off the Kerry coast, ▶ eight miles into the storm-tossed Atlantic. The smaller of the two is a bird sanctuary richly coated with guano.

29-32. *Skellig Michael*, the larger, was inhabited by monks during the early Christian era; they built a precarious stone path to the peak (*left*) and lived in beehive-shaped huts (*below*). Puffins (*right*) enjoy friendly relations with the rock's visitors, who come regularly during the summer months.

33-35. *Dingle*, northernmost of Kerry's peninsulas, is rich in antiquities. A church in Kilmalkedar (*left*), with its Romanesque doorway, dates from the twelfth century. Gallarus oratory, shaped like an upturned boat, is still perfectly preserved, even after a thousand years. Ruins of beehiveshaped buildings (*right*) are of unknown date.

36. *Blasket Islands*, off the tip of Dingle, have been deserted for the past twenty years, although former residents return from time to time to tend their sheep and to fish.

37. *Paddy and Sean O'Sullivan*, cousins of Maurice O'Sullivan, who wrote about island life, come back regularly at shearing time. Most of the island houses are now in disrepair, although the O'Sullivans keep theirs in good condition.

38. *Blasket Sound*, between Great Blasket Island and Dingle, is dreaded for its treacherous waters; in the sixteenth century, at least one of the vessels belonging to the attacking Spanish Armada was wrecked here.

40. *A dolmen* in the Burren (County Clare): known as "giants' graves," they are thought to be tombs built about five thousand years ago; capstones of some weigh as much as a hundred tons.

39. *Burren*, which means "stony district," is a descriptive name for the barren limestone landscape of the region, although rare mosses and flowers thrive in the deep natural fissures between the rocks.

73

41-43. *Aran Islands*, in Galway Bay on the extreme western fringe of Europe, are the home of independent-minded, close-knit, Gaelic-speaking communities. *Opposite*, a view of Kilronan, on Inishmore, the largest; old women on Inishmaan (*below* and *overleaf*) sport shawls they have knitted themselves.

◀44. *Dun-Aengus,* on Inishmore, is a huge fort backing onto a sheer cliff two hundred feet above the water; it has been described as "the most magnificent barbarian monument in Europe."

Fingers into the Atlantic

Along the west coast of Ireland lie dozens of inhabited islands and countless uninhabited ones, ranging in size from such comparatively large islands as Inishmore, of the Aran trio, which has a population of over a thousand, to High Island, off the coast of Donegal, whose owner and sole inhabitant (part-time) is the poet Richard Murphy.

The bleakest of all the islands are the Skelligs, which pierce the Atlantic eight miles off the Kerry coast. Their remoteness and inaccessibility—the sea here is notoriously treacherous—made the larger of the two an ideal spot for eremitic monks of the early Christian period. They built for themselves a small monastery, with beehive-shaped stone cells, which look now almost exactly the same as they did a thousand years ago, for the climate is mild and frostless and there is nobody to carry away the stones.

Visiting the Skelligs is an exciting and strange experience, like a voyage into some world of fantasy. Weather permitting, boatmen from Valentia Island or Port Magee take visitors out regularly in the summer. We left Valentia aboard Des Lavelle's boat in the company of a friend, Brian Covington, and a group of deep-sea divers. The water is very choppy, visibility low, and for two hours we pitch

IRELAND ♣

about in the small boat before the nearer, and smaller, of the two
Skellig islands comes into view: a sheer black rock rising from the
sea, its peaks and crags covered in white, as if an enormous pail of
paint has been tipped over it. The island is a bird sanctuary, inac-
cessible to man, and as one approaches one sees that the white
"paint" is actually a vast accumulation of guano. Elegant gannets
swoop and circle, then drop like stones into the water for fish; little
puffins buzz about, their small wings beating frantically, as though
the act of remaining airborne were a tremendous struggle.

Skellig Michael, the other island, is also girdled by sheer cliffs,
although here it is possible to land at a small concrete jetty, the same
point at which the monks of old would have disembarked from
their rowing or sailing craft. Three lightkeepers and countless sea
birds and rabbits make their home on the rock. Puffins, resting up
from their aerial struggle, waddle about like comic old gentlemen
in dinner jackets and appear so tame one feels one might stretch out
one's hand and pet them; as we climb up to the monastery, they
watch us cannily, perhaps considering how funny we look, and the
rabbits scuttle about the rocks and tufty grass.

The monks built a stairway up the cliff out of giant slabs of stone,
which we climb through swirling mists, passing peculiarly tortured
rock formations. At the top, we find the ancient stone huts of the
monastery surrounded by soft, brilliant green sea moss, which feels
like sponge underfoot. Five hundred feet below, the white-toothed
waves bite at the black rocks; in the distance, the bird sanctuary
looks like an enchanted castle, its craggy turrets dusted in white
snow. Lying back on luxurious moss mattresses and eating our
sandwiches, we listen to the cries of the birds. Brian identifies them
for us as petrels, guillemots, fulmars, gannets, terns, razor-bills, and

rock pipits. We have great admiration for his ornithological erudition.

I find it hard to imagine how monks ever survived on this barren rock. They constructed, it seems, small terraces on the cliff edge, using stone walls as supports, so that they could grow a certain amount of food; and perhaps they kept chickens and goats. There are two wells on the island, but no trees or turf; fuel, then, if the monks used it at all, had to be brought in by boat. Winters must have been almost unbearably bleak.

Brian and I climb to the Needle's Eye, the highest peak of the island. It is a perilous ascent, with some giddy glimpses down sheer cliff faces. During the middle ages, pilgrims would come to Skellig Michael for this unnerving experience, and at the very top they would stretch up, next to a seven-hundred-foot precipice, to kiss a cross that was carved on the highest pinnacle of the rock. When we reach the narrow peak, which commands a magnificent view of the rugged Kerry coast, I can just barely hold the camera steady enough to take a picture.

Delightful and fascinating is the Dingle Peninsula, one of the long fingers of County Kerry that jut out into the Atlantic. The tip of Dingle is a Gaelic-speaking region to which students of Irish come to hear the language as it should be spoken and to practice their own conversation. Dingle is also a treasury of historical remains: there are numerous ancient beehive huts, some of them still used by farmers to house livestock, while the upturned boat-shaped oratory at Gallarus is the most perfectly preserved example of its type in Ireland.

Lying off the extreme tip of the Dingle Peninsula are the Blasket Islands, the last parish before America and now uninhabited. One

IRELAND ♣

of the most remarkable things about the small community of Gaelic speakers who lived here until the early fifties is that three of them wrote books which have become minor classics: Thomas O'Crohan's *The Islandman,* Maurice O'Sullivan's *Twenty Years A-Growing,* and Peig Sayers's *Peig.* The books paint a vivid picture of life in this small island community: the storms and the wrecks that made up the islanders' everyday struggle against the sea, their hardships and their joys.

With Sean and Paddy O'Sullivan, cousins of the author, we row out to the Blaskets one fine July morning. The boat is a long black curragh, which the two brothers have made themselves in the age-old way of stretching canvas over a light wooden frame and covering it with tar. As they carry the curragh aloft down to the water, the frail vessel looks like the shell of a giant mussel—and it feels disconcertingly like a shell when we sit down in it. But once the oars are in place and the men begin to row, the boat becomes reassuringly stable, while its light construction permits it to ride high on the waves.

The Blasket Sound, so often rough and treacherous, is calm as we cross. Lying in the stern and feeling the water slipping beneath me, I trail a spinner and pull in three large pollock, a kind of cod. Paddy points out where the Santa María, a vessel of the Spanish Armada, went down nearly four hundred years ago; many of the fleet were wrecked on this rugged coastline and in recent years divers have salvaged weapons and jewelry as well as gold coins.

The abandoned houses, most of them now roofless, stare blankly at us as we approach after nearly an hour's hard rowing by the O'Sullivans. The island is treeless but carpeted with grass, emerald bright under the summer sun and cropped short by the grazing sheep, which the two brothers have come over to shear. We pull onto the concrete slipway and carry the boat out of reach of the tide.

Climbing up through the ruins of the ghost village, we find all the paths overgrown with grass. The O'Sullivans' house, in which both brothers were born and which is still in good condition, is now used to store nets and lobster pots. We sit for a time outside, in the warm sun, drinking tea and talking, although neither of the brothers speaks much English. They tell us that they love the island and would like to live here still. The men who did once were strong, they say, but it was hard work, and there was no pub to relax in, and life for the women too was difficult. "Fetch water every day. Mend nets. Milk cow. Make bread. Find seaweed. Very hard." Later, after pausing to photograph the dramatic cliffs, I set out barefoot to walk to the western end of the island. There are no roads, but neither are there any stones to cut my feet. An hour later I stand looking out over the Atlantic on the furthest outpost of Europe. The air sweeps in from across the ocean, pure as air ought to be.

But my thoughts are on the Blaskets, sad symbols of Ireland's impoverished and isolated west coast and of the dying Celtic world. Only two decades ago, this Gaelic-speaking community still fought for survival, trying to make do with their scanty natural resources, hampered by a lack of social amenities, and disturbed by a growing awareness of the outside world thrust upon them by the mass media. Their efforts were in vain, for when an island community gets so small that it can no longer support a teacher, or a doctor, or even a nurse, and when most of its young men and women have emigrated, then it has reached the point of no return. It can no longer look after its ill and aged or educate its children, so emigration escalates and soon the land is deserted. That has been the unfortunate fate of Great Blasket Island as well as of other islands, such as Gola, on this sad Atlantic fringe of Europe.

The Aran Islands, west of Galway Bay, though surely among the most rugged and desolate places man has chosen to live in, have escaped that fate. Their communities having survived so far, it seems unlikely that even the soft, persistent hand of the twentieth century will weaken them to the point of collapse. *Man of Aran* sharply dramatized the hardship of the island life, particularly in the scenes showing the curraghs coming in during a storm and the islanders building fields from seaweed and scraps of soil gleaned from cracks in the rock.

There are three Aran islands in all, and it is the largest, Inishmore, that we visit first. As we disembark, we are most impressed by the stoniness (carboniferous limestone, in fact), which gives a gray cast to the light, unlike that of the Blaskets, where emerald green was the predominant color. Low stone walls enclose small and irregularly shaped fields, forming a kind of giant stone web atop the barren, treeless land; the white-walled houses are built of stone; many of the fields themselves are filled with stones; stone monuments commemorating the island's dead stand beside the road; and most impressive of all are the massive stone forts built around two thousand years ago. The biggest of these is Dun-Aengus, which has been described by some historians as the "most magnificent barbarian monument in Europe." It consists of four concentric semicircles of fortifications backing onto a sheer cliff two hundred feet above the water. Facing an attacking army, the defenders of the fort, with such a precipice behind them, would, literally, fight to the last drop.

Along the perilous edges of the cliffs, the islanders move as casually as city people strolling on familiar sidewalks. Just as casually they climb down onto small ledges to gather birds' eggs. Some, using extremely long lines, fish from the cliff tops; when they make a catch, they spend the next five minutes hauling it up. Should a ship be wrecked at the foot of the cliffs, the islanders descend on ropes to rescue the survivors or to salvage wood that might be used in making furniture or frames for the curraghs.

Sixty years ago, J. M. Synge, the playwright, who lived for many years on Inishmaan, the middle island, wrote of Aran life: "Much of the intelligence and charm of these people is due to the absence of any division of labor, and to the correspondingly wide development of each individual, whose varied knowledge and skill necessitate a considerable activity of mind. Each man can speak two languages. He is a skilled fisherman and can manage a curragh with extraordinary nerve and dexterity. He can farm simply, burn kelp, cut out pampooties, mend nets, build and thatch a house, and make a cradle or a coffin."

Much the same description might be written today, with but a few exceptions. Slate, for example, is replacing thatch as roofing material; the burning of seaweed for kelp ash (formerly an important source of iodine and potassium) is no longer, so far as I could ascertain, carried out; and the islanders are now less dependent on their own resources than they were in Synge's time. Government welfare, tourism, and remittances from relatives "on the other side" have become supplementary sources of income. Nevertheless, the islanders seem less well disposed toward outsiders than their mainland cousins. As a man of Inishmore said to me, when I wanted to take his picture in a pub: "We're enough on the map as it is without turning the page of a newspaper and seeing yourself drinking a pint." Like the black-cloaked women of Kinsale, the men of Aran are, understandably enough, tired of being spied at through the lens of a camera.

Inishmaan, the middle island, is only just beginning to be touched by the twentieth century. There are four telephones on the island, two tractors, one car, and one television set. There are no hotels or official guest houses, and there is only one pub. The nearest doctor is on Inishmore; once a week a priest comes over from Inisheer, the little island. The population of Inishmaan hovers around 350, depending on how many people are overseas working. Few tourists visit the island, which is perhaps why we find the people friendlier than those of Inishmore.

We stay with Mrs. Faherty, the village postmistress, who has a clean white stone house. She gives us plenty of simple, wholesome food (mostly fish and potatoes, home-baked soda bread and tea), which we eat in a small dining room under the watchful eyes of the late President Kennedy and the Infant of Prague. Mrs. Faherty's brother Rory makes us a pair of pampooties, a kind of local moccasin of untanned cowhide; and we are tempted to buy a large many-colored shawl, which has been made by Mrs. Faherty's mother, of the type worn by the old women of the island. Aran women are great knitters, but Mrs. Faherty herself, whose husband was recently killed in an accident, has no time for it; she is kept busy enough running the post office and looking after her large family and her paying guests.

There is good singing to be heard all over Ireland, but we have heard none so pleasing as that in the pub of Inishmaan, where visitors from the mainland sing traditional Irish folk songs and islanders reply with throaty Gaelic ballads. Dara Beg, who is a builder by profession, doubles as poet and composer; he has his own songs about such subjects as the poteen boat from Connemara, the new airstrip being built on the island, or the shark washed ashore not long ago. Someone else sings a song about a man who goes to find work in England and wanders from farm to farm with his sickle, looking for a job; as he walks through the countryside, he swears that he will never work for English farmers again.

A man from Dublin sings another anti-English song that ends with the words "... and the English to hell!" This prompts me to sing a song in return, which causes the Dublin man to apologize. He says he had not realized there was an Englishman present. As we buy each other drinks, he explains carefully that it is not individual Englishmen he hates, only England itself. What matters, he goes on philosophically, is not a man's position but his principles.

Ceili is a Gaelic word that means, broadly speaking, a party or a gathering, and I have always had the idea that an Irish *ceili* must be a wild affair where enormous amounts of drink are consumed and passions grow enflamed. Perhaps this is sometimes true, but on the whole the *ceili* we attend at the Inishmaan community hall is much like any village dance—at least for most of the evening. Music is provided by a phonograph, and the dances range from old-fashioned waltzes to Irish reels. However, there is passion in the young men's eyes during "The Walls of Limerick," a dance whose main object seems to be to twirl around so fast that the girl in your arms is thrown to the ground.

Just before two in the morning, everybody rises for the Irish national anthem, after which the girls go to powder their noses and the boys stand about outside the hall. Shortly the girls emerge in groups of two and three, carefully linked arm in arm. The boys whistle and shout and pull at the girls' dresses, and the girls scurry past as though running a gauntlet. Then the boys follow, whistling and howling in the sturdy black Aran night.

Traveling through other sections of the west, we find ourselves in the midst of landscapes as desolate and stony as that of the Arans. In County Clare, in the region known as the Burren (which means "stony district"), stone walls enclose fields that seem to contain nothing more than wide, smooth slabs of flat limestone, while hills are bare granite, without a scrap of green. Between these vast natural paving stones are deep fissures in which grow rare mosses and flowers, some of Alpine and Mediterranean origin. The odd structure and extreme porosity of the rock account for numerous caves, hot springs, and lakes that appear or disappear overnight.

The southern part of Connemara is also a land of barren rock, and in West Donegal is the area known as the Rosses, which has always been an inhospitable place to live in, as one learns from the autobiography of Paddy Gallagher, who founded a successful cooperative movement in the region. His description of his childhood is a detailed, Dickensian, and highly interesting picture of Donegal at the turn of the century. Paddy himself was ten when he first went to the hiring market at Strabane, where he and his companions paraded in the streets like cattle for the farmers' inspection, flexing their muscles on demand. Paddy was hired as a laborer for a period of six months at a total wage of three pounds.

At Glencolumbkille, I fall into conversation with an elderly woman in front of her large house. "I have four sons and three daughters," she tells me. "One son lives in America, two in London, one in Dublin. All my daughters are married and live in England. One son is staying with me now—he came over to cut the turf—but he'll soon be going back to England."

♣ FINGERS INTO THE ATLANTIC

Someone who is doing his best to put an end to this sort of tragic family breakup is Glencolumbkille's priest, Father MacDyer. He has been the driving force behind such projects as the bringing of water and electricity into the houses, and he has formed a weaving cooperative, a craft center, and a folk village that he hopes will bring a "discreet" type of tourism to the area. These efforts at revitalizing the spirit of the community have met with considerable success and have helped stem the outflow of the population.

Although Father MacDyer claims to have no political bias, he tells me he believes that Christianity leads directly to socialism. He wants to form a voluntary agricultural commune in the area, but despite the fact that 112 out of 130 farmers support him, the government has quashed his plans. "They are frightened," says the priest, "that we might succeed."

The government's own efforts to stimulate industry in the area have not been completely successful. There are factories now for producing textiles, carpets, canned foods, plastic containers, and toys, among other things, but there is still not enough work for young people.

Fishing is also a major industry here, although it has declined since the nineteenth century. Killybegs has good harbor facilities, a fish-processing plant, and a boat-building enterprise. Further up the coast, on Aran Island (not to be confused with the three Arans), salmon fishing is very profitable during the season. At Mulhern's Corner Bar in Dungloe, the proprietor tells me that salmon is selling for nine shillings a pound, which averages out to over ten dollars a fish, and a boat with a crew of four or five men will net anywhere between six hundred and two thousand fish during the short two-month season, which adds up to a nice bit of change.

IRELAND ♣

It would be a mistake, then, to paint too bleak a picture of the west. Although it is certainly poor, my impression is not one of desperate poverty, and the days of the one-room cabin which the farmer and his family share with the cows and the poultry are over, for the government has granted generous subsidies to help people improve their living conditions. In a small pub near Rosaveel, however, when I ask where the toilet is, the landlord replies, "We don't have such here, but you may make use of the back lane."

The people of Aran Island, or Arranmore, as it is sometimes called, of whom there are just under a thousand, are proud of the fact that there are no resident police on the island. Once a year, a constable comes over from Burtenport across the water to fix up the dog licenses; otherwise the islanders enjoy a remarkable amount of self-government and freedom from the law. The men, in fact, joke about declaring themselves a republic and issuing their own stamps; they argue about who will be prime minister and who the chancellor. And they have plenty of time and places to argue in, for the pubs keep their own hours. I am amazed to see that they are still full of people with the coming of the dawn. "The pubs close when the last man leaves," I am told, "and the key is never turned in the lock." The island's one hotel, the Glenbay, continues serving breakfast until one o'clock in the afternoon.

I cannot help wondering, somewhat enviously, if Aran is ever visited by the tax collector. Yet if an island is a place of freedom, it is also in its way a prison. I discuss this paradox with Tommy Timoney, a man who was born on the island but who has spent most of his life abroad. Afflicted with an eye disease, he has returned for a last look at the place of his birth and his mother's grave.

Together he and I go to visit Mrs. Sheila Campbell, an old friend of his mother and one of the oldest inhabitants of the island. "Do you remember me, Sheila?" Tommy asks when the old woman comes to the door.

She peers closely at him. "No. I don't know who ye are."

"Look again, Sheila. You knew me well. And my mother and father."

"No, I don't know ye."

"My hair was red then, not white as it is now."

"I must be honest with ye—I don't know who ye are."

"It's Tommy Timoney, Sheila. Do you remember me now?"

The old woman's face breaks into a smile. "Tommy Timoney, you're a thousand times welcome. Come in, come in."

Soon I must catch the ferry back to Burtenport, so I leave Tommy and Sheila and her son Hughie reminiscing about old friends and old times. The subject has turned to a "great wake" they held for a friend long ago. "Yes," I hear old Mrs. Campbell say as I close the door softly behind me, "we Irish remember our dead."

If Ireland's fingers are the thin strips of land jutting out into the Atlantic from the rugged west coast, then the lakes and rivers are her soft heart, Cork and Galway are her nerve centers, and Belfast and Dublin are her brain. Throughout our trip, we have been reading of violence and destruction, of bombings and threats of bombings, of protest meetings and political manoeuvering. Is this, we wonder, the real Ireland?

We cross the border into Northern Ireland at Killeen, sixty-five miles north of Dublin and thirty-eight south of Belfast. Immediately we feel we have entered another country (in my case, my own). We pass a blown-up red telephone box by the side of the road; we know that we are in a troubled country.

IRELAND ♣

The border between the republic and Northern Ireland dates only from 1922, when the Irish Free State was formed in the south, and the Protestants in the north—urged on by Baron Caron and Lord Randolph Churchill (Sir Winston's father)—opted to remain as part of Britain rather than be ruled by a Catholic government in the south. Today the Protestants are still in the majority in the north, and the Catholics are an underprivileged minority. It is partly this discrimination against Catholics that provokes the present troubles, but there are many other causes, among them, the fervent Irish desire for a free and united republic, the traditional Irish hatred for the British, and a trend toward revolutionary socialism.

The part of northern Ireland that comes under the authority of the United Kingdom is often called Ulster, but the term is inaccurate: the province of Ulster consists of nine counties, of which only six are in the north. Like most borders, that which divides Ireland is wholly arbitrary. There are regions on the republic's side of the border that are predominantly Protestant, while many areas on the other side are mostly Catholic.

The border is open, except of course to arms smugglers and members of the outlawed I.R.A., but at the same time it is not well guarded, as the successes of the republican extremists demonstrate. When we go through, on the eve of the big parades and celebrations that mark the anniversary of the Battle of the Boyne, there is an exodus of caravans and holiday cars steering toward the south and away from trouble.

It is Sunday, and the wide streets of Belfast are empty save for an occasional platoon of troops or marching Orangemen getting ready for the morrow's parades. In the late evening bonfires are lit in Protestant areas all over the city in preparation for the stroke of midnight and the beginning of the glorious day. In the best of circumstances, it would seem unnecessary to celebrate a battle fought so long ago, but now the celebrations are almost unbelievably tactless. They can only aggravate the bitterness and the hatred.

Midnight strikes. It is the 281st anniversary of the victory of Protestant William over Catholic James, and the bonfires rage as fiercely as though the victory had only just been won. Boys and girls of the Protestant persuasion, like the drummers and pipers of William's army, march about the fires and sing their old songs, changing the words so as to make obscene comments about the Pope. At this moment, this high point of the victorious ecstasy, there comes a dull thud from the direction of the city center, as if City Hall has been picked up by a giant hand and thumped down again. A sudden hush falls over the crowds. Explosions are heard all too often in Belfast, but still, "What's gone now?" people ask. A few moments later there is another thud, then still another: the I.R.A. has poisoned the victory wine.

The next day, as the Orangemen parade through the streets wearing orange-colored sashes and black bowler hats they can hardly avoid seeing the blown-out windows of the main post office and of a large department store. In the afternoon a British sentry is shot dead. At Finnagay's Field, the Reverend Martin Smyth, an extreme right-wing Protestant, speaks to the assembled marchers, calling for armed retaliation against the Catholics. I bring out my camera to take a photograph of the Reverend Martin Smyth, but I am prevented by the Orangemen about me; when I try to write down what he is saying, the page is ripped from my notebook.

My wife and I come to the obvious conclusion that Belfast is, for the time being, no place for an extended stay, so we drive around

IRELAND ♣

the Antrim coast to Londonderry (or Derry, as the Catholics call it), stopping briefly on the way to photograph the Giant's Causeway and Dunluce Castle. The coastline itself is a beautiful one, but the weather does not favor us.

Londonderry once must have been a handsome city, but now the the old walls are cloaked with barbed wire, and bombed buildings have been bricked up. This, I overhear someone say, is a peaceful afternoon for Derry; there must be something good on television. To me, as I suppose to almost all visitors who come to Northern Ireland, both sides seem to have lost almost all semblance of reason. Most Irishmen we speak to are sick of the "troubles," and many fear that civil war is inevitable. It appears that there is a plethora of ideas for the solution of the problems, the only point of agreement being that there is no easy answer.

It is with a sense of relief that we recross the border. Once back to the soft, green heart of Ireland, fishing for trout on the dark waters of Loch Derg, the only troubles in our minds are caused by the fish, which are not biting this evening. As the late sun casts a flickering, golden flame across the lake, I reflect that Ireland with her tears and tragedy, joy and peace, humor and hospitality, will always be Ireland.

46-47. *Horsemanship* (both riding and breeding) is a skill of which the Irish are extremely proud, and their deep love for their horses is an ancient one. Young riders at a country meeting (*overleaf*) take their racing as seriously as the professional jockeys at Galway (*above*).

48-49. *Hurling*, a game similar to hockey, is Ireland's national sport and one at which legendary heroes excelled. Teams, which once numbered two hundred, are now limited to fifteen.

50. *Music* is a universal pastime in Ireland: of ancient origin but as alive now as ever, it greets the visitor everywhere and makes him wish his own musical standards were as high.

51. *Ceili*, a Gaelic word meaning a gathering, is the country's main social event, with dances ranging from the traditional to the modern. *Above*, a *ceili* on Inishmaan.

53. *Connemara*, a district ▶ in the west of Galway, is famous for the beauty of its many lakes. *Overleaf*, the crystal clear water of Lough Muck on a fine summer's day.

52. *A cowboy* uses a bicycle to move cattle from one of his two small fields to the other, ten miles away. The scene is County Galway, in the west of Ireland.

103

54. *Ponies* on a bleak bog near Derryrush huddle together for warmth; these hardy and finely marked animals are indigenous to the region.

55-57. *W. B. Yeats*, one of the century's greatest poets and perhaps the greatest Irish poet of all, died in the south of France in 1939, and after the war his body was brought back to Ireland to lie (as he had desired) in the churchyard at Drumcliff, in County Sligo. *Left*, Drumcliff Bay, of which the poet wrote: "There midnight's all a glimmer, and noon a purple glow . . . ."

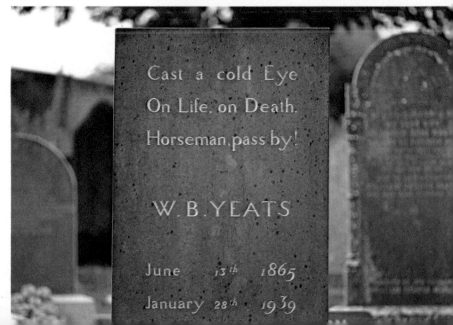

Cast a cold Eye
On Life, on Death.
Horseman, pass by!

W. B. YEATS

June 13th 1865
January 28th 1939

58-60. *County Donegal*, in the northwest, is one of Ireland's loveliest regions. *Above*, Arranmore, an island just off the coast with a population of under a thousand, is a major salmon fishing center. *Left*, a donkey, a symbol of old Ireland, shares parking space with a modern car in Donegal town. *Opposite*, a fishing boat at Arranmore, with the Donegal coastline and Mount Errigal in the background.

◀61. *Antrim coast* of Northern Ireland is the rugged background for the Giant's Causeway, created by rapidly cooling lava.

62. *Near the ruins* of Dunluce Castle lie the wrecks of several ships of the Spanish Armada.

63. *Strange carvings* of early Christian saints and church fathers have stood vigil on remote White Island in Lough Erne (County Fermanagh) for over a thousand years.

64. *Belfast parade* of Orangemen celebrates the defeat of ▶
Catholic James by Protestant William—way back in 1690.
Protestant domination of Northern Ireland belies its
small majority.

65. *A shrine* in the Bogside, Londonderry, marks the spot where a young Catholic was shot by British troops. Can there ever be peace in a divided Irish nation?